Date _____

Sweet numbers

CW00793288

Know what each digit in a number up to 100 stands for

● coloured pencils

Fantastic Fizzers Factory!

| 45 | 20 | 33 | 34 | 18 | 27 |

three tens

two tens

one ten

8 units

4 units

7 units

two tens

5 units

4 tens

0 units

3 units

three tens

Teacher's notes

Look at the tens and units on the sweets and match the sweets to the jars to which they belong. Now colour each pair of sweets to match the jars.

3

Date _____

Seaside numbers

- **Read and write numbers to 100**

Teacher's notes

In each row, look at the numbers written in words. In the spaces on the flags, buckets and kites, write the numbers in figures.

Date_____

Counting kangaroos

Continue a number pattern and recognise odd and even numbers

You need:
- coloured pencils

12   Count on in 1s

16   Count on in 2s

15   Count on in 5s

30   Count on in 10s

HOME

Teacher's notes

Top: Count on in ones, twos, fives or tens from each of the 2-digit numbers shown.
Bottom: Colour the stones showing even numbers only, to show the stones that the kangaroo needs to land on to reach its home.

Date_____

Spaceships and stars

● Order numbers up to 100

Teacher's notes

Look at the number on each spaceship. On the star to the left of the spaceship, write a number that is smaller. On the star to the right of the spaceship, write a number that is larger.

Date_____

Milkshake money

● **Solve problems about money**

 13p  15p  10p 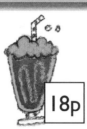 18p 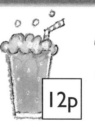 12p  17p

---

Ella bought  and

| 12p | + | 10p | = | 22p |

Tom had 20p. He bought

| 20p | ◯ | ☐ | ◯ | ☐ |

Imran bought  and

| ☐ | ◯ | ☐ | ◯ | ☐ |

Naomi had 25p. She bought

| ☐ | ◯ | ☐ | ◯ | ☐ |

Megan bought  and

| ☐ | ◯ | ☐ | ◯ | ☐ |

Leon had 30p. He bought

| ☐ | ◯ | ☐ | ◯ | ☐ |

Teacher's notes

Look at each problem in turn. Choose the most appropriate addition or subtraction operation to solve each one. Write each calculation in the spaces provided.

Date _____

Save and spend

● Solve problems about money

Ella has 20p.

Ella buys a cake.

 20p (−) 5p (=) [ ]

She buys a pencil.

[ ] (−) [ ] (=) [ ]

Gran gives Ella 10p.

[ ] (+) [ ] (=) [ ]

Ella buys a balloon.

[ ] ( ) [ ] ( ) [ ]

She finds 5p!

[ ] ( ) [ ] ( ) [ ]

She gives her
brother 10p.

[ ] ( ) [ ] ( ) [ ]

... and his birthday presents!

Teacher's notes

8 Follow Ella as she spends and saves her money. Look at each problem and write each as a calculation.
Keep a running total throughout.

Date_____

Calculating cats

- Add and subtract one-digit and two-digit numbers

You need:
- coloured pencils

21 + 5   25 + 4   33 + 5

19 – 4   27 – 3   35 – 4

9 – 4 = 5   5 – 4 = 1   5 + 4 = 9

7 – 3 = 4   1 + 5 = 6   3 + 5 = 8

 31    29    15

 26   24    38

Teacher's notes
Choose the number fact shown on the cat flaps that can be used to solve the calculation on each cat.
Colour the flap to match the cat's collar and then colour the bowl showing the correct answer.

9

Date _____

Computer calculations

● Understand that addition and subtraction 'undo' each other

| 0 | 1 | 2 | 3 | 4 | 5 | 6 | 7 | 8 | 9 | 10 |

2 + 3 = 5

5 – 3 = 2

4 + 6 = ☐

☐ – ☐ = ☐

1 + 7 = ☐

☐ – ☐ = ☐

6 + 0 = ☐

☐ – ☐ = ☐

3 + 3 = ☐

☐ – ☐ = ☐

5 + 4 = ☐

☐ – ☐ = ☐

5 – 1 = ☐

☐ + ☐ = ☐

8 – 5 = ☐

☐ + ☐ = ☐

2 – 1 = ☐

☐ + ☐ = ☐

4 – 2 = ☐

☐ + ☐ = ☐

10 – 10 = ☐

☐ + ☐ = ☐

9 – 4 = ☐

☐ + ☐ = ☐

Teacher's notes

10

Look at the calculation at the top of each pair. Using the number track at the top to help you count on or back in ones, complete the calculation and write it in the box. Now write the corresponding addition or subtraction fact underneath.

Date _____

Gecko guesses

● Estimate a group of objects

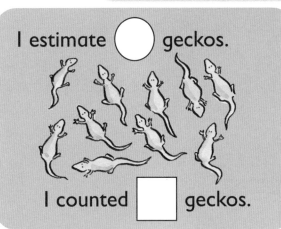

I estimate ⬭ geckos.

I counted ☐ geckos.

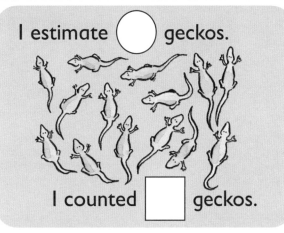

I estimate ⬭ geckos.

I counted ☐ geckos.

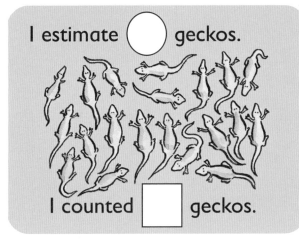

I estimate ⬭ geckos.

I counted ☐ geckos.

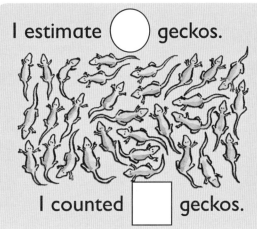

I estimate ⬭ geckos.

I counted ☐ geckos.

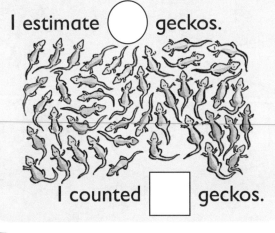

I estimate ⬭ geckos.

I counted ☐ geckos.

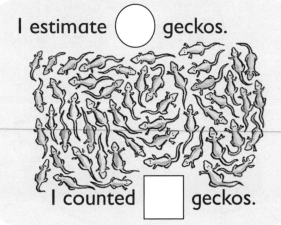

I estimate ⬭ geckos.

I counted ☐ geckos.

Teacher's notes

Look quickly at each group of geckos in turn. Then cover the picture with your hand and write your estimate in the circle. Then count the actual number of geckos and write your answer in the box.

Date _____

Addition detective

● Know addition facts for numbers to 10

3 + ☐ = 5

1 + ☐ = 1

2 + 1 = ☐

☐ + 1 = 2

2 + ☐ = 4

4 + ☐ = 7

6 + ☐ = 9

3 + ☐ = 6

☐ + 4 = 8

2 + ☐ = 10

Teacher's notes

The detective is looking for the missing number in each addition calculation. Write the missing number in each number sentence to complete the addition calculations.

Date _____

Submarine subtraction

Know subtraction facts for numbers to 10

You need:

● coloured pencils

 5

 8 − 6

 6 − 5

6

 8 − 2

 2

 9 − 4

1

 10 − 1

8

 10 − 2

 3

 7 − 3

9

 10 − 3

10

 10 − 0

4

 9 − 6

7

Teacher's notes

Work out the calculation on each submarine. Colour the fish with the correct answer the same colour as the submarine.

Date_____

Clever calculations

Know addition and subtraction facts to 10

7 + 2 = ☐

10 − 6 = ☐

2 + 4 = ☐

7 − 4 = ☐

6 + 4 = ☐

9 − 2 = ☐

3 + 4 = ☐

6 − 4 = ☐

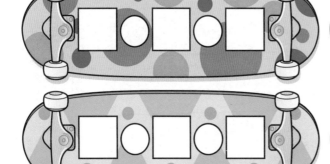

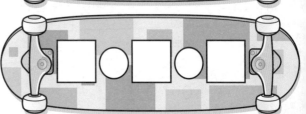

Teacher's notes

14

Answer each addition and subtraction fact. Then match each addition fact to the related subtraction fact by colouring the skater's T-shirt to match the skateboard showing the appropriate subtraction fact. Underneath, write four more related calculations on the skateboards, matching them according to colour

Date _____

Doubles and halves

- Know doubles of numbers to 20 and the matching halves

You need:

- coloured pencils

Teacher's notes

Complete each of the routes by drawing a line to join them, finding the doubles of numbers 1 to 6, and the halves of numbers 2, 4, 6, 8, 10, 12. Then colour the trees and house along each route the colour of the 'double' house at the start.

15

Date_____

Painting by numbers

- **Use knowledge of number facts and operations**

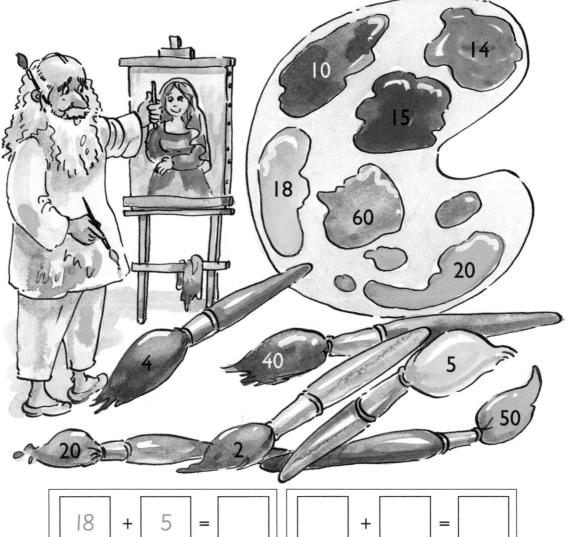

| 18 | + | 5 | = | | | | + | | = | |

| | + | | = | | | | + | | = | |

| | + | | = | | | | + | | = | |

Teacher's notes

Match the colour of each paintbrush to the paint on the palette. Write the two numbers as an addition calculation then complete the sum. Remember to put the larger number first.

Date _____

Pocket money problems

- Solve problems about money

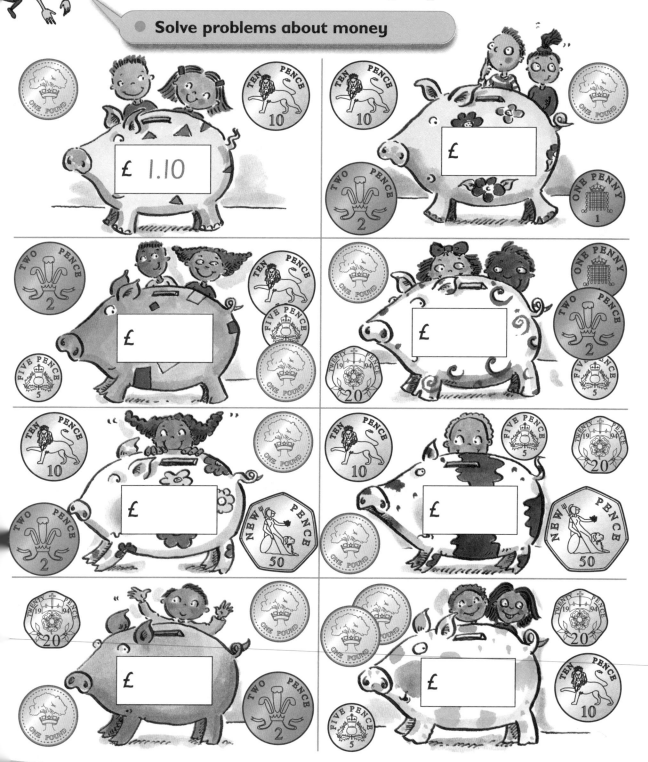

Teacher's notes

Look at each child or pair of children and work out how much pocket money they have altogether.
Write this total on the money box.

Date _____

Pounds and pence

- **Solve problems about money**

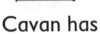

Cavan has [   ]

Erin has [   ]

Meena has [   ]

Caie has [   ]

How much do Cavan and Caie have altogether? [   ]

How much do Meena and Erin have altogether? [   ]

Who can buy this book?  £2.00 [   ] and [   ]

Who can only buy this comic?  £1.10 [   ] and [   ]

Teacher's notes

Look at the amount of money each child has and write the amount in the box. Use this information to solve the problems underneath.

Date _____

Odds and evens treasure

Describe patterns and relationships

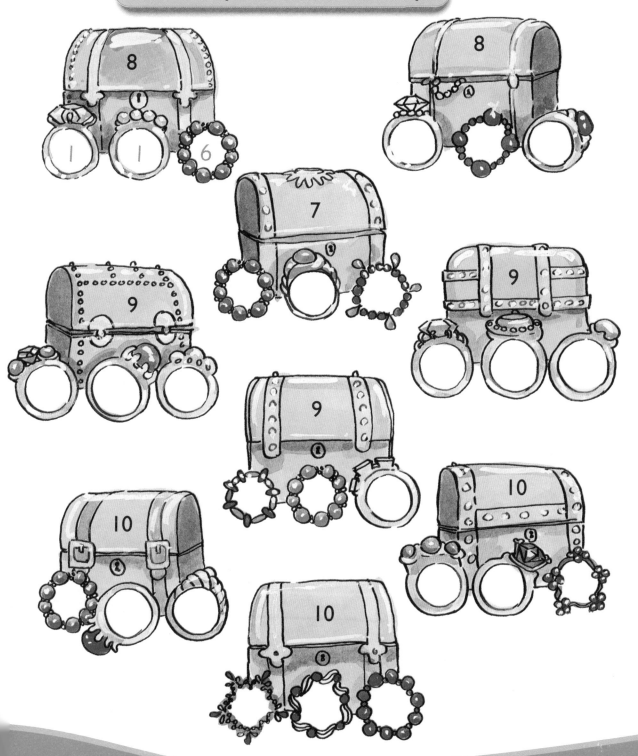

Teacher's notes

Look at the number on each treasure chest. Write odd numbers in the gold rings and even numbers in the beaded rings to make the total on the chest. Each total must be made up in a different way.

Date _____

Propeller problems

● Describe patterns and relationships

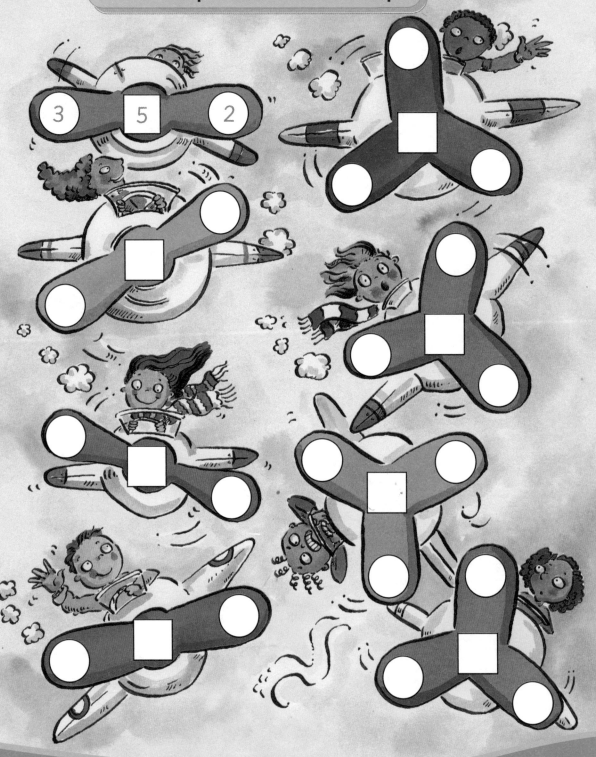

Teacher's notes

On each aeroplane propeller, write 2, 3, 4 or 5 in the circles and write the total in the box.
Make as many different calculations as you can. You can use the same number twice.

Date _____

Picnic problems

Solve word problems

Tom has bought 14 chicken rolls and 12 salad rolls.

| 14 | + | 12 | = | 26 | rolls |

Tom drops 4 on the way!

| 26 | − | 4 | = | 22 |

Tom has [ ] rolls left.

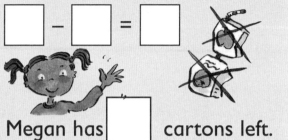

Ayesha has 13 packets of cheese crisps and 16 packets of plain crisps.

| [ ] | + | [ ] | = | [ ] | packets |

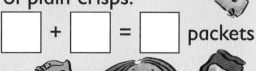

She buys 3 more on the way!

| [ ] | + | [ ] | = | [ ] |

Ayesha has [ ] packets of crisps.

Megan has 15 cartons of apple juice and 17 cartons of orange.

| [ ] | + | [ ] | = | [ ] | cartons |

She and Leona drink 2 of them!

| [ ] | − | [ ] | = | [ ] |

Megan has [ ] cartons left.

Marcus has 13 saltfish patties and 12 vegetarian patties.

| [ ] | + | [ ] | = | [ ] | patties |

He collects 10 more.

| [ ] | + | [ ] | = | [ ] |

Marcus has [ ] patties altogether.

Teacher's notes

Write the correct numbers into each addition or subtraction calculation and then work out the answer to each problem.

Date_____

Names of shapes

● Look at pictures of 2-D shapes and name them

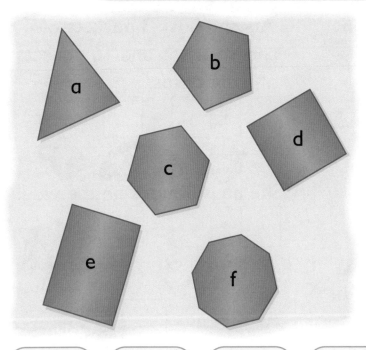

a	*triangle*
b	
c	
d	
e	
f	

◯ triangle ◯ square ◯ rectangle ◯ pentagon ◯ hexagon ◯ octagon ◯

Teacher's notes
Write the name of each shape.

22

Date _____

Pinboard shapes

● **Make 2-D shapes using a pinboard**

Draw 3 different triangles

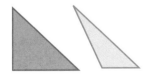
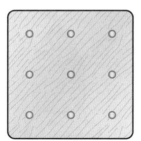

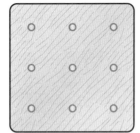
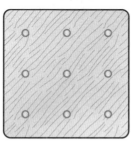

Draw 3 different squares and rectangles

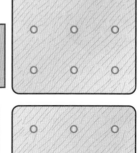

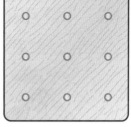

Draw 3 5-sided shapes

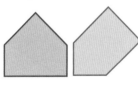

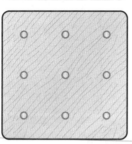

Draw 3 6-sided shapes

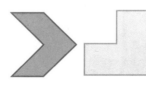
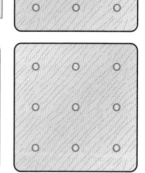

A 5-sided shape is called a

A 6-sided shape is called a

Teacher's notes

Follow the instructions and draw different shapes on the pinboards. You can copy the examples given or make up your own shapes. Complete the sentences at the bottom of the page.

Date _____

Shapes at the fair

● Look at pictures of 3-D solids and match them

Teacher's notes

24 Look at the fairground objects and the shapes that are on them. Draw lines to connect the different fairground shapes to their solid shapes.

Date_____

Magician shapes

● **Name 3-D solids and describe them**

cone cube sphere cylinder pyramid cuboid

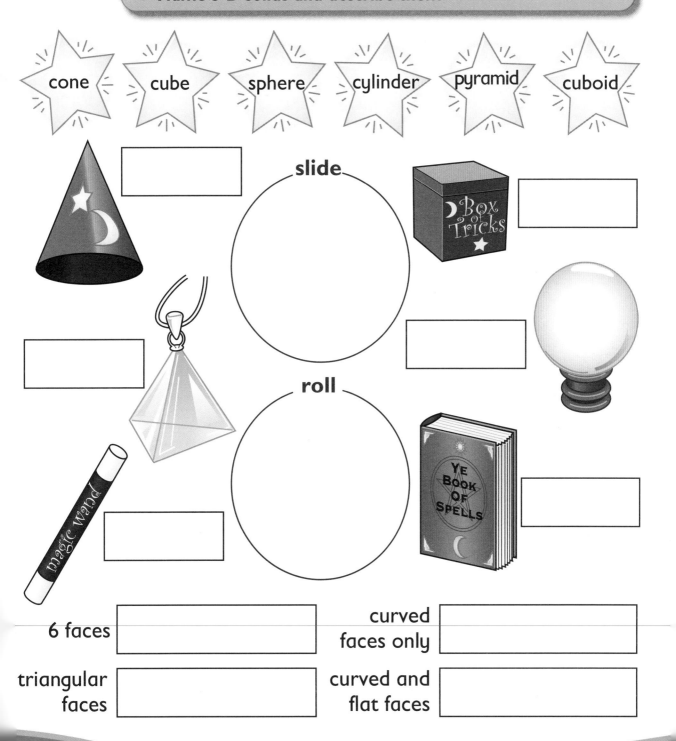

slide

roll

6 faces		curved faces only	
triangular faces		curved and flat faces	

Teacher's notes

Top: Write the name of the shape. Draw a line to join each shape to the correct sorting circle.
Bottom: Look at the faces of each shape and write its name in the correct box.

25

Date_____

Daily choices

● **Solve a puzzle involving time**

You need:
● coloured pencils

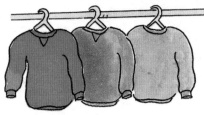

Monday	Tuesday	Wednesday

Thursday	Friday	Saturday	Sunday

Teacher's notes

26

Can Ashrif wear a different combination of sweatshirts and trousers every day of the week?
Colour his sweatshirts red, purple or orange, and his trousers blue or black to find out.

Date _____

Mobile measurements

● **Estimate, measure and compare lengths using centimetres**

You need:
● 10 interlocking 1 cm cubes

Object	Length of string	
	Estimate	Measure
moon	4 cm	5 cm
planet	cm	cm
sun	cm	cm

Object	Length of string	
	Estimate	Measure
rocket	cm	cm
star	cm	cm
spaceman	cm	cm

The shortest string is ____cm, then ____cm, then ____cm,

then ____cm, then ____cm, and the longest is ____cm.

Teacher's notes

Estimate the length of each string in centimeres. Write it down. Make a rod of centicubes to check and write the actual measurement. Beginning with the shortest, order the lengths of string.

Date _____

Estimate and measure

Estimate, measure and compare lengths using centimetres

You need:
- ruler
- objects to measure

Things to measure	Estimate	Measure
length of a lunch box	20 cm	about 21 cm
	cm	cm
	cm	cm
	cm	cm
	cm	cm
	cm	cm

Teacher's notes
Estimate the length of a lunch box. Then measure the lunch box using words like: **about**, **nearly**, **close to**. Now find five more things to estimate and measure and write them in the spaces provided.

Date_____

How high is it?

● **Read a simple scale marked in 10s**

about 20 cm

_____ cm

_____ cm

_____ cm

Teacher's notes

In each picture there is an object and a measuring stick. Read the height of the object to the nearest 10 cm and write your answer underneath. Use words like: **about, nearly, close to**.

29

Date_____

Sorting sweets

● **Sort objects and say how they were sorted**

10	Not 10

There are ☐ sweets marked with a 10.

White	Not white

There are ☐ sweets that are not white.

_____	Not _____

Teacher's notes

Cross off each sweet and draw it in the correct side of each of the top two diagrams. Complete the sentences. Now choose a different way to sort the sweets. Write the headings in the bottom diagram. Cross off the sweets again and sort them into your table.

Date _____

Shape sorting

● **Put information in tables**

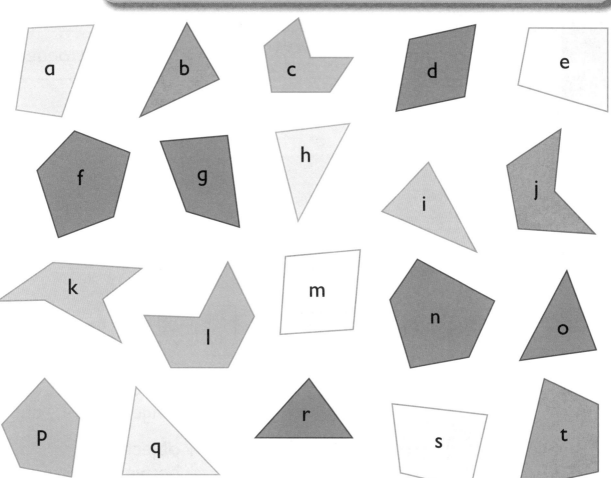

a   b   c   d   e   f   g   h   i   j   k   l   m   n   o   p   q   r   s   t

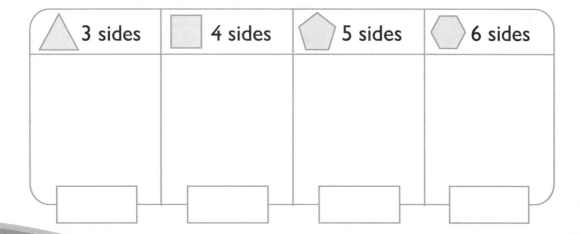

△ 3 sides	▢ 4 sides	⬠ 5 sides	⬡ 6 sides

Teacher's notes
Look at each shape and count the number of sides. Write the shape's letter in the correct column.
Write the total number of each shape in the box.

Date_____

Sorting objects by length

- **Sort objects and say how they were sorted**
- **Find if something is longer or shorter than a given length**

10 cm or shorter	Between 10 cm and 20 cm	20 cm or longer

20 cm

10 cm

This pencil is between 10 cm and 20 cm long

You need:
- 15 classroom objects

☐ objects are 20 cm or longer.

☐ objects are longer than 10 cm.

☐ objects are between 10 cm and 20 cm long.

☐ objects are shorter than 20 cm.

☐ objects are **not** shorter than 20 cm.

There are ☐ objects altogether.

Teacher's notes

The red strip is 20 cm long. The blue strip is 10 cm long. Find 15 objects and compare their lengths with the red and blue strips. Write their names in the correct set. Count the objects in each set and write the number in the box. Complete the sentences.

Date _____

Egg sorter

• **Sort numbers in different ways**

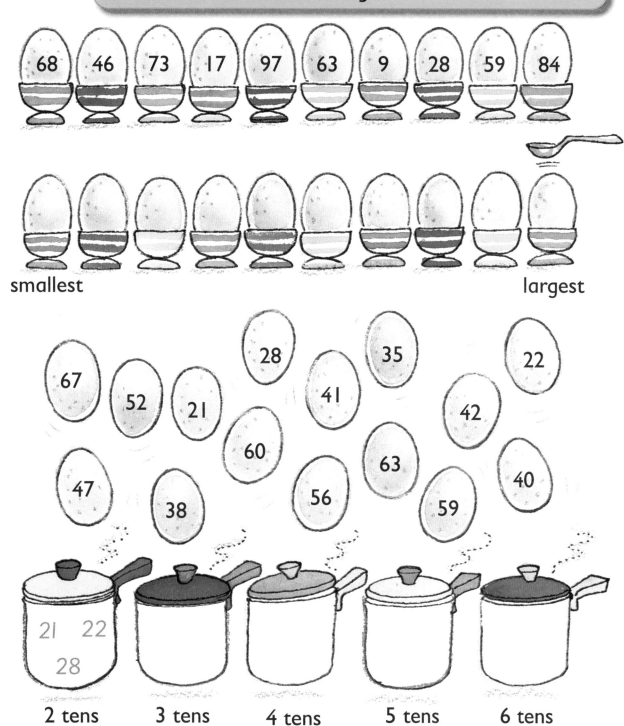

68 46 73 17 97 63 9 28 59 84

smallest   largest

67 52 21 28 41 35 22
47 38 60 56 63 59 42 40

2 tens	3 tens	4 tens	5 tens	6 tens
21 22 28				

Teacher's notes

The top row of eggs are in the wrong order. Write the numbers in the correct order underneath, from smallest to largest. Now sort the next set of eggs according to their tens and write them in the correct pan.

33

Date_____

Flower sorting

• **Sort and order numbers**

You need:
• yellow and orange pencils

Odd Numbers

Even Numbers

Which is the largest odd number? [ ]

Which is the largest even number? [ ]

Teacher's notes

34

Look at the flowers. Colour the centres with even numbers yellow and those with odd numbers orange.
Sort the numbers into odds and evens, starting with the smallest numbers. Complete the sentences.

Date _____

Sort the whistles

- **Use tables to show information**

You need:
- ruler

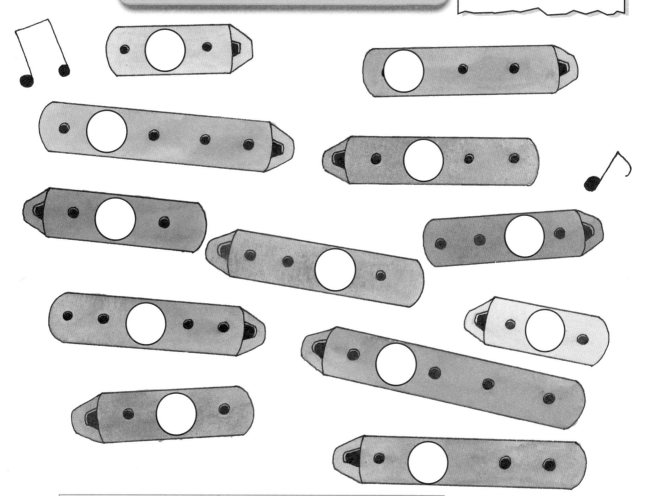

Whistle length	Number of whistles
4 cm	
5 cm	
6 cm	
7 cm	
8 cm	

Teacher's notes
Measure the length of each whistle and write the number of centimetres in the circle on the whistle.
Now complete the table.

Date_____

Sorting books

● **Use tables to show information**

You need:
● selection of different books

Shorter than Activity Book	Taller than Activity Book
☐	☐

☐ books are shorter than the Activity Book.

There are ☐ books altogether.

Number of words in each title

Shortest ←——————————————————→ Longest

☐ titles have 3 words.

The most common number of words is ☐

Teacher's notes

Compare the heights of different books with this Activity Book and complete the table and sentences. Write down the number of words in each title, from the shortest to the longest and complete the sentences.

Date_____

Bridging through 10

● **Add any pair of one-digit numbers**

| 5 | 5 | | 9 | 1 | | 6 | 4 | | 7 | 3 |

= 13

10 + 3

6 + 4 + 3

6 + 7

= ☐

10 + 1

☐ + ☐ + 1

5 + 6

= ☐

10 + 2

☐ + ☐ + 2

7 + 5

= ☐

10 + 5

☐ + ☐ + 5

9 + 6

Teacher's notes
Complete each bridge by choosing the correct number bond for 10 from the top of the page.
Write the answer to the sum on the top of the bridge.

Date _____

Bridging through 10 sails

● **Add any pair of one-digit numbers**

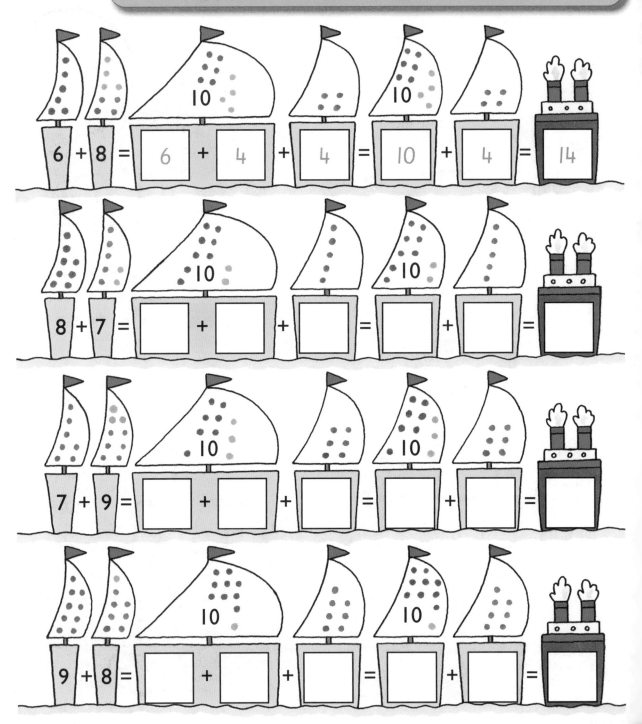

6 + 8 = 6 + 4 + 4 = 10 + 4 = 14

8 + 7 = ☐ + ☐ + ☐ = ☐ + ☐ = ☐

7 + 9 = ☐ + ☐ + ☐ = ☐ + ☐ = ☐

9 + 8 = ☐ + ☐ + ☐ = ☐ + ☐ = ☐

Teacher's notes

Look at the different-coloured dots on the sails. Write the number fact for each addition number sentence. Then complete the sequence and write the total on the ship.

Date_____

10 and 20

● Add or subtract a one-digit number to or from 10 and 20

You need:

● coloured pencils

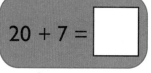

$20 + 7 = \boxed{}$

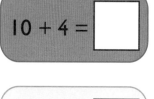

$10 + 4 = \boxed{}$

$10 + 6 = \boxed{}$

$10 + 3 = \boxed{}$

Hide 3!

$10 - \boxed{} = \boxed{}$

Hide 7!

$20 - \boxed{} = \boxed{}$

Hide 4!

$20 - \boxed{} = \boxed{}$

Teacher's notes

Top: Count the fingers and thumbs on each child and write the number on their shirt. Find the calculation which matches. Shade their shirts the same colour. Then complete each calculation.
Bottom: Look at the instructions and complete the calculations.

Date _____

Apple and cherry tens and units

● **Add a one-digit number to a 'tens' number**
● **Subtract a one-digit number from a 'tens' number**

10 + 7 =

20 + 4 =

20 + 9 =

30 + 9 =

30 + 3 =

20 − 4 = 16

20 − 7 =

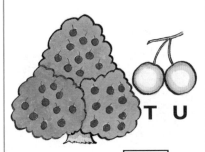

30 − 5 =

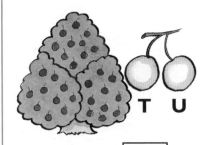

30 − 8 =

Teacher's notes

40

Look at each pair of apple trees. On the first tree, colour the number of apples to show the tens. On the second tree, colour the number of leaves to show the units. For each cherry tree, cross out the number of cherries that have fallen off and write the remaining cherries as tens and units. Complete each calculation.

Date _____

Boot sale bridging

- Add a one-digit number to any two-digit number
- Solve problems

Erin bought a car for 14p and a comic for 7p

14	(+)	7
14	(+)	6 (+) 1
20	(+)	1 = 21

Erin spent ☐ p altogether.

Leon bought a dinosaur for 9p and a drum for 13p

☐	◯	☐
☐	◯	☐ ◯ ☐
☐	◯	☐ = ☐

Leon spent ☐ p altogether.

Theo bought a book for 18p and sweets  for 5p

☐	◯	☐
☐	◯	☐ ◯ ☐
☐	◯	☐ = ☐

Theo spent ☐ p altogether.

Mia bought a pencil for 6p and a teddy  for 19p

☐	◯	☐
☐	◯	☐ ◯ ☐
☐	◯	☐ = ☐

Mia spent ☐ p altogether.

Teacher's notes

Read each word problem. Show each stage of bridging through 20 to work out the answer to each one.

41

Date _____

How long is it?

● **Draw and measure lines to the nearest centimetre**

You need:
● a ruler

C

E

B

Measure
how long
it is:

A

from star A to star C _____12__ cm

from star C to star D _____ cm

from star D to star B _____ cm

from star B to star E _____ cm

D

from star E to star A _____ cm

Teacher's notes

Using a ruler, draw a line to join the centre of star C to the centre of star D. Measure the length of the line in centimetres and write down your answer. Do the same with the other stars.

Date_____

Pet show problems

● **Decide what calculation to do to solve a problem**

door: 20 cm   mesh: 30 cm

How long is
the rabbit hutch? ☐ cm

Sophie's pony is
80 cm tall. Cath's is 12 cm taller.

How tall is Cath's pony? ☐ cm

The water was 11 cm deep.
I added 3 cm more.

How deep is
the water now? ☐ cm

The 70 cm lead is ☐ cm
longer than the 60 cm lead.

Teacher's notes
Solve the word problem in each picture and write the answer in the space provided.

43

Date _____

Collection times

• Tell the time when it is o'clock or half past the hour

half past 8 in the morning

1 o'clock in the afternoon

half past 6 in the evening

1 hour

Collection times
11:30 morning
3:00 afternoon
7:30 evening

10:30 in the morning

2 hours

12:00 in the afternoon

3 hours

half past 4 in the afternoon

Teacher's notes
Look at the times on the letters and the postbox. Decide how many hours there are to the next collection time for each letter, then join the letter to the correct hour box.

Date_____

In one minute...

You need:
- minute timer
- items for each task

- Estimate how long an activity might take, then check using a timer

In one minute I can...		Estimate	Measure
draw round a triangle		☐ times	☐ times
join a cube to another one		☐ cubes	☐ cubes
bounce a ball		☐ times	☐ times
put a peg on a washing line		☐ pegs	☐ pegs
thread a bead on a lace		☐ beads	☐ beads
write my name		☐ times	☐ times

Teacher's notes

Work in pairs. Guess the number of times you can do each task in one minute. Write it down in the Estimate box. Now do the task when your partner says 'go'. Record the actual number of time in the Measure box.

45

Date_____

In position

● **Follow and give instructions to mark a position on a grid**

circle is in | B3 | triangle is in | |

square is in | | rectangle is in | |

pentagon is in | | hexagon is in | |

Put a cross in square B2.

Put a tick in square C1.

Find the seat for Emma | | Josh | | Jim | | Carol | |

Write who is sitting in seat A1 | | seat C2 | |

seat B3 | | seat D1 | |

Teacher's notes

46 Find the shape/child in the square/grid. Write the letter below and the number to the left to give the position of the shape/child.

Date _____

Friendly addition

- **Identify and record information**
- **Work out the unknown number in a number sentence**

0 1 2 3 4 5 6 7 8 9 10 11 12 13 14 15 16 17 18 19 20 21 22 23 24 25 26 27 28 29 30

19 + 5 = 24
Name _Ellis_____

9 + ☐ = 18
Name _____

10 + 6 = ☐
Name _____

15 + ☐ = 27
Name _____

13 + 7 = ☐
Name _____

17 + ☐ = 30
Name _____

 24 Ellis

 22 Amir

 16 Sam

 25 Caie

 13 Ayesha

 12 Cavan

 20 Samira

 8 Naomi

 17 Tommy

 9 Megan

Teacher's notes

To find out which friends Farah is visiting, complete each of the addition calculations. Use the number line to help you. Write the name of the friends Farah visits under each calculation.

47

Date_____

Supermarket subtraction

● **Work out the unknown number in a number sentence**

You need:

● coloured pencils

washing powder

baked beans

apples

$16 - 5 = \boxed{11}$

$\boxed{} - 12 = 4$

$22 - 8 = \boxed{}$

$\boxed{} - 19 = 5$

$26 - \boxed{} = 3$

$29 - 4 = \boxed{}$

okra

bread

toothpaste

Teacher's notes

48

To find out which item was bought by each child, complete each of the subtraction number sentences on the trolleys. Now colour each trolley to match the star by the item bought.

Date _____

Castle calculations

You need:
● coloured pencils

● **Work out the unknown number in a number sentence**

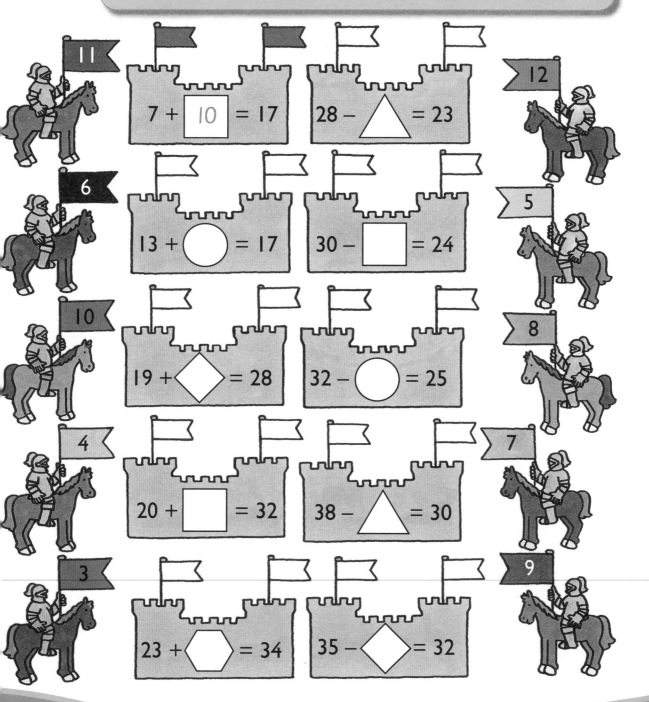

11

7 + [10] = 17

28 − △ = 23

12

6

13 + ◯ = 17

30 − ☐ = 24

5

10

19 + ◇ = 28

32 − ◯ = 25

8

4

20 + ☐ = 32

38 − △ = 30

7

3

23 + ⬡ = 34

35 − ◇ = 32

9

Teacher's notes

Look at the calculation on each castle and write in the missing number. Now colour the turret flags to match the knight's flag that shows that missing number.

Date_____

Freezies ices

● **Find one half of sets of objects**

You need:
● coloured pencils

Put ice cream on to half of these cornets.

Half of 6 is 3 .

These are strawberry and lemon ice lollies. Colour half of them pink and half yellow.

Half of [ ] is [ ] .

Draw a spoon with half of these ice cream tubs.

Half of [ ] is [ ] .

Put a flake into half of these ice creams.

Half of [ ] is [ ] .

Half of these lollies should have chocolate on them. Colour half of the lollies brown.

Half of [ ] is [ ] .

Teacher's notes

50 Read the instructions for each picture, then draw or colour as required.
Now complete the sentence underneath.

Date _____

Quick quarters

● **Find one quarter of shapes and sets of objects**

You need:
● coloured pencils

Colour $\frac{1}{4}$ of each pizza.

Colour $\frac{1}{4}$ of each cake.

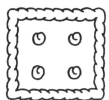
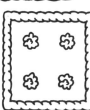

Colour $\frac{1}{4}$ of these tins of beans.

Colour $\frac{1}{4}$ of these apples red. Colour the rest green.

Colour $\frac{1}{4}$ of these sausages.

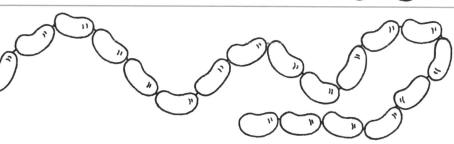

Teacher's notes
Read the instructions for each picture, then colour as required.

51

Date_____

Jam tart multiplication

● Show repeated addition as multiplication

| 1 | set of 2 → | 2 |

| | sets of 2 → | |

| | sets of 2 → | |

| | sets of 2 → | |

| | sets of 2 → | |

| | sets of 2 → | |

| | sets of 2 → | |

| | sets of 2 → | |

Teacher's notes

The Queen of Hearts bakes tarts in sets of two. On each tray draw a set of two tarts.
Write how many sets of two there are, then write how many tarts there are altogether.

Date_____

Birthday twos

● **Show repeated addition as multiplication**

You need:

● coloured pencils

 = 4

candles

 1 × 2

 = ☐

candles

2 × 2

 = ☐

candles

3 × 2

 = ☐

candles

4 × 2

 = ☐

candles

5 × 2

 = ☐

candles

6 × 2

7 × 2

 = ☐

candles

 = ☐

candles

8 × 2

Teacher's notes

Look at each plate and write the number of candles in the space provided. Now colour each plate to match the party hat showing the correct calculation.

53

Date _____

Jam tart division

- **Show sharing as division**

| 2 | tarts shared |

between 2 knaves

is ☐ each.

☐ tarts shared

between 2 knaves

is ☐ each.

☐ tarts shared

between 2 knaves

is ☐ each.

☐ tarts shared

between 2 knaves

is ☐ each.

☐ tarts shared

between 2 knaves

is ☐ each.

Teacher's notes

54

Share the tarts on the big tray equally between the two knaves and draw the correct number of tarts on each tray. Write how many tarts are being shared and how many each knave has in the spaces provided.

Date_____

Divided space

Use the symbols ÷ and = to record number sentences

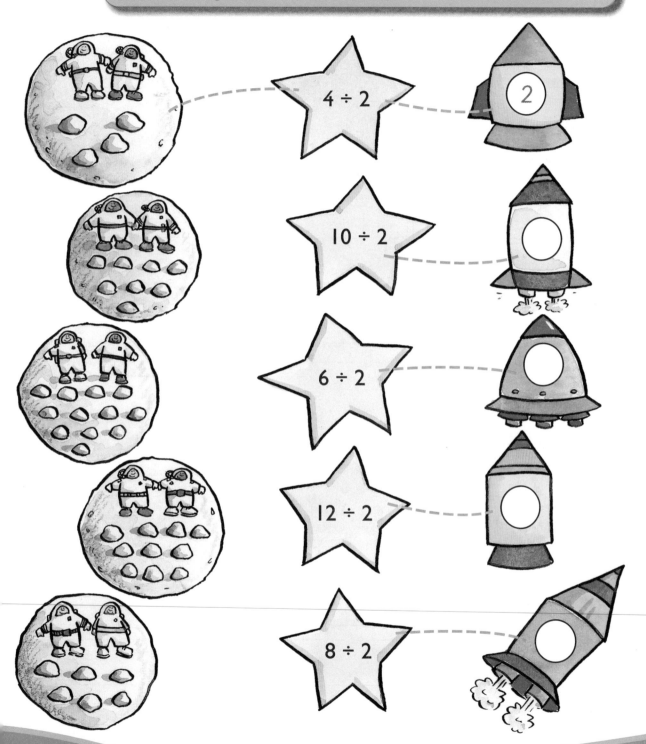

Teacher's notes

Work out how many rocks each spaceman will carry to the spaceship when they are shared equally.
Draw a line to the correct calculation. Write the answer on the spaceship.

Date _____

Doubling machines

● **Know all doubles up to 20**

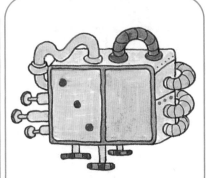

4 + 4 = 8

4 × 2 = 8

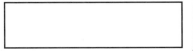

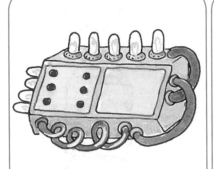

Teacher's notes

56

Double the number of buttons shown on each machine, writing an addition and multiplication fact for each.

Date _____

Multiply by 2

● Know the 2 times table and recognise multiples of 2

Teacher's notes
Look at the multiplication fact on each sunflower and join it to the bee showing the correct answer.

Date _____

Multiply by 5

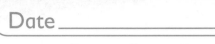

● Know the 5 times table and recognise multiples of 5

$3 \times 5 =$

$7 \times 5 =$

$4 \times 5 =$

$8 \times 5 =$

$9 \times 5 =$

$6 \times 5 =$

$10 \times 5 =$

$2 \times 5 =$

$1 \times 5 =$

Teacher's notes

58

Look at the multiplication fact on each surfboard and write the answer on each swimmer.

Date _____

Multiply by 10

● **Know the 10 times table and recognise multiples of 10**

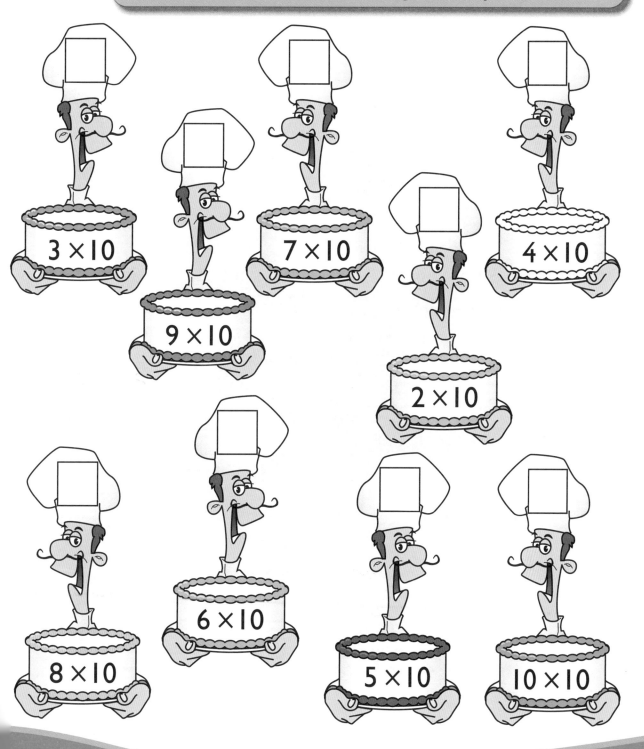

3×10

9×10

7×10

4×10

2×10

8×10

6×10

5×10

10×10

Teacher's notes

Look at the multiplication fact on each cake and write the answer on each chef's hat.

Date _____

Problem page

● **Solve problems**

Leon buys 10 flowers.

He gives half to his mum and half to his dad.

$\boxed{} \div \boxed{} = \boxed{}$

They have ___ flowers each.

Yee has 2 plates of cakes.

Each plate has 4 cakes on it.

$\boxed{} \times \boxed{} = \boxed{}$

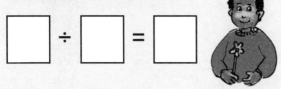

Yee has ___ cakes.

Ben has 2 bug boxes.

He has 3 bugs in each one.

$\boxed{} \times \boxed{} = \boxed{}$

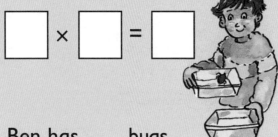

Ben has ___ bugs.

Megan has 8 toy cars.

She keeps half in a green box and half in a red box.

$\boxed{} \div \boxed{} = \boxed{}$

She has ___ cars in each box.

Ali has 12 cherries.

He shares them equally with his sister.

$\boxed{} \div \boxed{} = \boxed{}$

They have ___ cherries each.

Erin has 2 hens.

Each hen has laid 5 eggs.

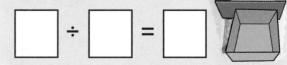

$\boxed{} \times \boxed{} = \boxed{}$

Erin collects ___ eggs.

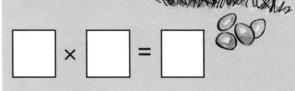

Teacher's notes

Read each word problem then write the multiplication or division calculation in the spaces provided. Now complete the sentence underneath.

Date _____

Garden problems

● Choose and use the right operation when solving word problems

2 ladybirds have 6 spots each.

How many spots do they have altogether?

☐ ○ ☐ = ☐

There are 10 petals on this flower.

Half of them fall off.

How many petals are left?

☐ ○ ☐ = ☐

There are 8 snails.

They are divided equally between 2 leaves.

How many snails on each leaf?

☐ ○ ☐ = ☐

There are 2 plants.

10 butterflies are around each plant.

How many butterflies?

☐ ○ ☐ = ☐

There are 10 earthworms in the 2 window boxes.

How many earthworms are in each?

☐ ○ ☐ = ☐

2 spiders have 8 legs each.

How many spiders' legs altogether?

☐ ○ ☐ = ☐

Teacher's notes

Read each word problem then write the multiplication or division calculation in the spaces provided.

Maths Facts

Number

0 1 2 3 4 5 6 7 8 9 10 11 12 13 14 15 16 17 18 19 20

Place value

100	200	300	400	500	600	700	800	900
10	20	30	40	50	60	70	80	90
1	2	3	4	5	6	7	8	9

Addition and subtraction facts to 10

0
$0 + 0 = 0$ $0 - 0 = 0$

1
$1 + 0 = 1$ $1 - 1 = 0$
$0 + 1 = 1$ $1 - 0 = 1$

2
$2 + 0 = 2$ $2 - 2 = 0$
$1 + 1 = 2$ $2 - 1 = 1$
$0 + 2 = 2$ $2 - 0 = 2$

3
$3 + 0 = 3$ $3 - 3 = 0$
$2 + 1 = 3$ $3 - 2 = 1$
$1 + 2 = 3$ $3 - 1 = 2$
$0 + 3 = 3$ $3 - 0 = 3$

4
$4 + 0 = 4$ $4 - 4 = 0$
$3 + 1 = 4$ $4 - 3 = 1$
$2 + 2 = 4$ $4 - 2 = 2$
$1 + 3 = 4$ $4 - 1 = 3$
$0 + 4 = 4$ $4 - 0 = 4$

5
$5 + 0 = 5$ $5 - 5 = 0$
$4 + 1 = 5$ $5 - 4 = 1$
$3 + 2 = 5$ $5 - 3 = 2$
$2 + 3 = 5$ $5 - 2 = 3$
$1 + 4 = 5$ $5 - 1 = 4$
$0 + 5 = 5$ $5 - 0 = 5$

6
$6 + 0 = 6$ $6 - 6 = 0$
$5 + 1 = 6$ $6 - 5 = 1$
$4 + 2 = 6$ $6 - 4 = 2$
$3 + 3 = 6$ $6 - 3 = 3$
$2 + 4 = 6$ $6 - 2 = 4$
$1 + 5 = 6$ $6 - 1 = 5$
$0 + 6 = 6$ $6 - 0 = 6$

7
$7 + 0 = 7$ $7 - 7 = 0$
$6 + 1 = 7$ $7 - 6 = 1$
$5 + 2 = 7$ $7 - 5 = 2$
$4 + 3 = 7$ $7 - 4 = 3$
$3 + 4 = 7$ $7 - 3 = 4$
$2 + 5 = 7$ $7 - 2 = 5$
$1 + 6 = 7$ $7 - 1 = 6$
$0 + 7 = 7$ $7 - 0 = 7$

8
$8 + 0 = 8$ $8 - 8 = 0$
$7 + 1 = 8$ $8 - 7 = 1$
$6 + 2 = 8$ $8 - 6 = 2$
$5 + 3 = 8$ $8 - 5 = 3$
$4 + 4 = 8$ $8 - 4 = 4$
$3 + 5 = 8$ $8 - 3 = 5$
$2 + 6 = 8$ $8 - 2 = 6$
$1 + 7 = 8$ $8 - 1 = 7$
$0 + 8 = 8$ $8 - 0 = 8$

9
$9 + 0 = 9$ $9 - 9 = 0$
$8 + 1 = 9$ $9 - 8 = 1$
$7 + 2 = 9$ $9 - 7 = 2$
$6 + 3 = 9$ $9 - 6 = 3$
$5 + 4 = 9$ $9 - 5 = 4$
$4 + 5 = 9$ $9 - 4 = 5$
$3 + 6 = 9$ $9 - 3 = 6$
$2 + 7 = 9$ $9 - 2 = 7$
$1 + 8 = 9$ $9 - 1 = 8$
$0 + 9 = 9$ $9 - 0 = 9$

10
$10 + 0 = 10$ $10 - 10 = 0$
$9 + 1 = 10$ $10 - 9 = 1$
$8 + 2 = 10$ $10 - 8 = 2$
$7 + 3 = 10$ $10 - 7 = 3$
$6 + 4 = 10$ $10 - 6 = 4$
$5 + 5 = 10$ $10 - 5 = 5$
$4 + 6 = 10$ $10 - 4 = 6$
$3 + 7 = 10$ $10 - 3 = 7$
$2 + 8 = 10$ $10 - 2 = 8$
$1 + 9 = 10$ $10 - 1 = 9$
$0 + 10 = 10$ $10 - 0 = 10$